Uniquely Pennsylvania

Susan McCulloch

Heinemann Library
Chicago, Illinois

**Library of Congress
Cataloging-in-Publication Data**

McCulloch, Susan H., 1968–
    Uniquely Pennsylvania / Susan McCulloch.
    p. cm. — (Heinemann state studies)
Includes bibliographical references and index.
    ISBN 1-4034-4496-X (lib. bdg.) —
ISBN 1-4034-4511-7 (pbk.)
    1. Pennsylvania—Juvenile literature. [1. Pennsyl-
vania.] I. Title. II. Series.
    F149.3.M33 2003
    974.8—dc21

                                    2003009424

Acknowledgments
Development and photo research by Book Builders
LLC

The author and publishers are grateful to the
following for permission to reproduce copyright
material:

Cover photographs by (top, L-R) Lindsay
Hebberd/Corbis; Joseph Sohm, ChromoSohm
Inc./Corbis; Joseph Nettis/Photo Researchers Inc.;
AFP/Corbis; (main) Dave Bartruff/Corbis

Title page (L-R); Blair Seitz/Photo Researchers Inc.;
Mark C. Burnett/Photo Researchers Inc.; Richard A.
Cooke/Corbis; contents page Joseph Nettis/Photo
Researchers Inc.; p. 4 Courtesy Elfreth's Alley Associ-
ation; p. 5 Mark Burnett/Photo Researchers Inc.;
p. 6 Andre Jenny/Alamy Images; pp. 8, 11T, 18
Bettman/Corbis; pp. 9, 42, 45 International Map-
ping Associates; p. 10 Courtesy Children's Hospital
of Pittsburgh; p. 11B Luca DiCecco/Alamy Images;
p. 12 Courtesy the Philadelphia Zoo; p 13T Joseph
Sohm, ChromoSohm Inc./Corbis; p. 14 Bonnie
Sue/Photo Researchers Inc.; p. 15T Martin B.
Withers, Frank Lane Picture Agency/Corbis; p. 15B
Gregory K. Scott/Photo Researchers, Inc.; p. 16T
Photo Researchers Inc.; p. 16M Hans Reinhard/
Bruce Coleman Inc.; p. 16B Darwin Dale/Photo
Researchers Inc.; p. 20 Van Bucher/Photo
Researchers Inc.; p. 21, 22, 43M Culver Pictures;
p. 23 Philadelphia Museum of Art/Corbis; p. 24
Underwood & Underwood/Corbis; pp. 25, 41
AP/Wide World Photos; p. 26 Courtesy Hershey
Community Archives; pp. 29, 37 Reuters
NewMedia Inc./Corbis; pp. 30, 33 Blair Seitz/Photo
Researchers Inc.; p. 31 Lindsay Hebberd/Corbis; p.
32 Bob Krist/Corbis; p. 34 Fred Hebegger/Grant
Heilman Photography; p. 35 R. Capozzelli/ Heine-
mann Library; p. 36 J. Irwin/H. Armstrong Roberts;
p. 38T Courtesy Pennsylvania State University; p.
38B Len Redkoles/Philadelphia Flyers; p. 39 Jeff
Greenberg/Estock Photo; p. 40 AFP/Corbis; p. 43T
Dave Bartruff/Corbis; p. 43B Joseph Nettis/Photo
Researchers Inc.; p. 44 Richard A. Cooke/Corbis

Special thanks to Jessica Elfenbein of the University
of Baltimore for her comments in the preparation
of this book.

Every effort has been made to contact copyright
holders of any material reproduced in this book.
Any omissions will be rectified in subsequent
printings if notice is given to the publisher.

Some words are shown in bold, **like this.**
You can find out what they mean by looking
in the glossary.

Contents

Uniquely Pennsylvania

There are 50 states in the United States. All belong to one country, but each state is unique in its own way. A state's special blend of history, geography, people, and culture makes it different from the others, or unique.

One way that Pennsylvania is unique is its history. Pennsylvania is called the **Keystone** State. As a keystone supports the foundation of a building, Pennsylvania supported the foundation of the early United States. This was largely due to its location in the center of the Thirteen Colonies. Leaders from the six colonies to the north and six colonies to the south met in Pennsylvania to discuss the direction of the new United States.

PHILADELPHIA

In Philadelphia, the largest city in the state, the 1700s blend with the 2000s. On one side of the city is Elfreth's Alley, the country's oldest residential street, dating back to 1702. In the center of town is City Hall, the world's

Elfreth's Alley was named for Jeremiah Elfreth, a blacksmith who owned much of the property there in the 1700s.

largest **municipal** building, built at the beginning of the 1900s. Branching out from City Hall is the Benjamin Franklin Parkway, lined with modern museums. And at the end of the parkway lies Fairmount Park, the largest U.S. city park, which covers 4,180 **acres**.

PITTSBURGH

Pittsburgh became the state's second largest city, thanks to the **Industrial Revolution** (1700s). In 1875 a man named Andrew Carnegie (1835–1919) built the world's largest steel mill, U.S. Steel, previously called Carnegie Steel Corporation. At that time, Pittsburgh was already a successful port, with steamboats and barges traveling its rivers. Also, the Pennsylvania Railroad created a path across the Allegheny Mountains, for easier access to the west. Carnegie and other business leaders saw the benefit of building factories at such an ideal spot. For the next hundred years, Pittsburgh was the nation's leader in steel making.

City of Brotherly Love

William Penn, the founder of Pennsylvania, came to America so he could freely practice his religion. As a member of the Quaker religion, he faced fines and imprisonment for his beliefs in England. When he came to present-day Pennsylvania, he started a community where people of all religions, colors, and beliefs could live together in peace. Because of Penn's practices, Philadelphia became known as the City of Brotherly Love.

Pittsburgh sits where three rivers come together—the Ohio, the Allegheny, and the Monongahela (muh-NON-guh-HAY-luh). Pittsburgh's factories depend on these rivers for shipping cargo to other states.

When steel manufacturing slowed down in the 1960s and 1970s, Pittsburgh began to change. For example, the first heart, liver, and kidney transplants were performed at Presbyterian University Hospital in Pittsburgh.

HARRISBURG

Harrisburg grew from a small country town to a capital city. In 1705 John Harris Sr. built a cabin and a ferry along the Susquehanna River in the center of the state. He used the river to carry people, food, and supplies to other towns. Before long his trading post was known as Harris's Ferry. In 1785 this growing city became Harrisburg. Because of its location along the Susquehanna River in the center of the colonies, it almost became the nation's capital. In the end, Harrisburg lost the honor to Washington, D.C. But Harrisburg did become the state's capital in 1812. Today, about 52,000 people call Harrisburg home.

In 1979 Harrisburg made news around the world for another reason. Ten miles away, a nuclear power plant called Three Mile Island had the biggest and most expensive **nuclear** accident in U.S. history. Nuclear power is not created by fuels such as coal or oil but by reactions made inside **atoms**. This reaction creates a large amount of heat and pressure, which is controlled by huge 12-feet thick towers. A pipe in one of the reactors began to leak, and the workers tried hard to stop it. Nevertheless the heat and pressure was so great that **radiation** escaped.

The accident at Three Mile Island cost $1 billion to clean up.

Pennsylvania's Geography and Climate

Pennsylvanians splash in mountain lakes in the summer. In the fall they enjoy the changing leaves. In winter they bundle up and hit the ski slopes. And in spring they watch the daffodils bloom.

THE LAND

There are three main geographic regions in Pennsylvania. The Atlantic Coastal Plain covers much of the southeast and is made up of flatland, small hills, and rivers. The Delaware River flows through this region.

Groundhog Day

Every February 2, Americans turn to Punxsutawney (punk-suh-TAW-nee) Phil for weather advice. Phil is not a weather forecaster. Phil is a groundhog who lives in Punxsutawney, Pennsylvania.

For more than a century, the town has followed an old German tradition of watching a local groundhog's reaction when he climbs out of his hole. If Phil is scared by his shadow, he ducks back in to **hibernate**. According to legend, this means six more weeks of winter is on the way. If Phil does not see his shadow, spring is on its way.

Johnstown Flood

The 1889 Johnstown Flood was one of the worst natural disasters in U.S. history. On May 30, 1889, a rainstorm soaked Johnstown, a city that lies in a valley surrounded by three rivers—the Conemaugh, the Little Conemaugh, and the Stony Creek. The rain caused the rivers to overflow. The walls of the South Fork Dam broke, and 20 million tons of water reaching 40 feet high and a mile wide poured into the city. The flood washed away buildings and bridges, killing 2,209 people.

    Americans around the country shipped food, clothing, lumber, and money to Johnstown. Even Clara Barton came to help victims find shelter. Barton (1821–1912) was a famous **Civil War** (1861–1865) nurse who founded the American Red Cross.

It is the second busiest in the country. Every year, boats carry more than 70 million tons of cargo in and out of the river's ports! At sea level, the Delaware also marks the lowest point in the state.

This flat coastal land rises into the hills and fertile farms of the Appalachian Plateau. The plateau covers the western half of the state and winds through the Pocono and Allegheny mountains. The state's highest point sits on this plateau. Mount Davis, in Somerset County, rises 3,213 feet above sea level.

The ups and downs of the Appalachian Plateau reach all the way to the western end of the state. Here, the land slopes down to the shores of Lake Erie. Called the Great Lakes Plain, this flat region borders Ohio.

THE WEATHER

Pennsylvania has a **temperate** climate. Its location places it in the path of air masses from the midwest, as well as from the Atlantic Ocean, and even the Gulf of Mexico. These changing forces create variety in the weather. The state enjoys four distinct seasons. The average temperature in January is 22 to 32°F. In July the temperature is usually 66 to 76°F.

People living in western Pennsylvania see more snow than those in the east, thanks to the higher altitudes of the Allegheny, Blue, and Laurel mountain ranges. Erie, in the northwest, gets around 54 inches a year. Meanwhile, Allentown, in the southeast, averages only 30 inches a year.

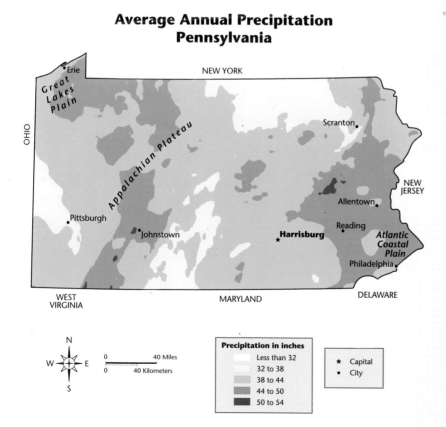

Average Annual Precipitation Pennsylvania

The annual amount of rain in Pennsylvania is 42 inches. This and the mild spring and summer make for a long growing season. Farmers in the North can grow crops for about 130 days a year. People in the Southeast can tend crops for up to 170 days.

Famous Firsts

HERE'S TO OUR HEALTH

In the 1950s polio affected more than 57,600 people in the United States. Polio is a **virus** that causes fevers, limps, and **paralysis**. To protect people from this serious illness, Dr. Jonas E. Salk, of the University of Pittsburgh, worked on a **vaccine** for eight years. After much testing and research, Salk's vaccine was introduced to the public. Within a few years, polio was no longer a threat.

In 1971 a simple idea began to save people all over the world. People at the Poison Center at Children's Hospital of Pittsburgh designed a character called Mr. Yuk. Bright green stickers with his face warned children to stay away from poisonous detergents, cleaners, and polish. In 2001, 42 million stickers were used in the United States, Europe, and Asia.

When this scowling face was tested on children, one child said, "Ooooh, that's yucky." And the name Mr. Yuk *was born.*

DON'T CHANGE THAT CHANNEL!

In the early 1900s, Dr. Frank Conrad, an engineer at the Westinghouse Corporation in Pittsburgh, had an idea. He wound up his Victrola, an old record player, and played it into his radio microphone. Back then radios were used only for listening to talking. So when people heard music, they were excited. Westinghouse heard about Conrad's broadcasts and built a radio station in 1920 to reach more people. Called KDKA, the station sent radio waves out for miles. It was the first commercial radio station in the United States.

KDKA's first broadcast, or live program, aired on November 2, 1920. It announced the results of the presidential election. In the coming years KDKA would be the first in the nation to broadcast a religious service and a baseball game. People still tune in to KDKA today.

Another Pittsburgh station, WQED-TV, is also a famous first. In 1954 stations were owned by companies and advertisers. WQED was the first station owned by the community. Because Pittsburgh citizens gave money to WQED, they helped decide what types of programs would air. The main goal of WQED was to educate, so it created shows such as the *National Geographic* specials and *Where in the World Is Carmen San Diego?* The station has won 60 **Emmy Awards** for excellence in television.

Mister Rogers' Neighborhood was one of the first programs to air on WQED. Fred Rogers left his job at NBC in New York to devote himself to educational television. He died in 2003.

SOMETHING TO CHEW ON

In 1928 Walter Diemer was playing with recipes at the Fleer Chewing Gum Company, in Philadelphia. By accident Diemer created a stretchy, bubbly batch. He added the one food dye color he had—pink—and went out to sell the first bubble gum. When he blew bubbles, the public was hooked. Diemer called the gum Dubble Bubble, and to this day it still has its original flavors—a mix of wintergreen, peppermint, vanilla, and cinnamon.

OTHER FAMOUS FIRSTS

Though born in Boston, Benjamin Franklin (1706–1790) contributed much to Pennsylvania. In 1731 Franklin founded the Library

Diemer was proud of his invention. He once said, "I've done something with my life. I've made kids happy around the world."

The Philadelphia Zoo protects many endangered animals, including Chaka, a silverback gorilla.

Company of Philadelphia, the first **circulating library** in the United States. Today, the library is famous for its collection of old, hard-to-find books, including the original drawings of the artist Beatrix Potter. Some of the more than half-million books date back as far as the 1400s.

In 1874, 3,000 people visited the Philadelphia Zoological Gardens. This was the first time in the United States that wild animals were put on display. Back then the zoo housed 282 animals, including 5 American black bears. Today, more than 1,600 animals live in the zoo. Many are **endangered** and rare, including the zoo's African white lions.

The first American department store was Wanamaker's, which opened in Philadelphia in 1876. It was the first store to sell a wide variety of products, not just one type. A few years later, Woolworth's, the first successful chain store, opened in Lancaster in 1879. Other stores carrying the Woolworth name would soon open in other cities. By 1911, there were a total of 1,000 stores.

The Baltimore Orioles played the Pittsburgh Pirates in the first World Series night game. Game Four was played on October 13, 1971, in Pittsburgh's Three Rivers Stadium. The Pirates won with a final score of 4 to 3.

Pennsylvania's State Symbols

PENNSYLVANIA STATE FLAG

This blue and gold banner has been the official state flag since 1799. An American bald eagle, symbolizing freedom, sits on top of the state shield. The sailing ship represents commerce, or business, on Pennsylvania's many rivers. The plow and wheat are symbols of Pennsylvania's farmlands. The crossed olive branch and cornstalk stand for peace and prosperity, or success.

The state motto appears on the coat of arms: "Virtue, Liberty and Independence."

PENNSYLVANIA STATE SEAL

When a document carries this seal, it means that the paper is legal and official. The Pennsylvania state seal is divided into five parts:

- Sailing ship (commerce)
- Plow (rich natural resources)
- Sheaves of wheat (fertile fields)
- A cornstalk and an olive branch (peace and prosperity)
- Bald eagle (freedom)

The Pennsylvania state seal has been used since 1791.

"Pennsylvania"

Pennsylvania, Pennsylvania,

Mighty is your name,

Steeped in glory and tradition,

Object of acclaim,

Where brave men fought the foe of freedom,

Tyranny decried,

'Til the bell of independence filled the countryside.

Chorus

Pennsylvania, Pennsylvania,

May your future be filled with honor everlasting
  as your history.

Pennsylvania, Pennsylvania,

Blessed by God's own hand,

Birthplace of a mighty nation,

Keystone of the land.

Where first our country's flag unfolded,

Freedom to proclaim,

May the voices of tomorrow glorify your name.

State Song: "Pennsylvania"

"Pennsylvania" became the official state song in 1990. Eddie Khoury wrote the words, and Ronnie Bonner wrote the music.

State Flower: Mountain Laurel

In 1933 the Pennsylvania House and Senate were having a difficult time choosing the state flower. Governor Gifford

The mountain laurel is a green shrub with spikes of pink or white flowers. The blooms spot Pennsylvania mountainside every June.

Pinchot wanted the azalea, but the legislature preferred the pink mountain laurel. The governor finally asked his wife to decide, and she chose the laurel.

The eastern hemlock can grow to be 100 to 150 feet tall, and as wide as 6 feet in diameter.

STATE TREE: EASTERN HEMLOCK

The eastern hemlock was a welcome sight for Pennsylvania's early settlers. They used this plentiful tree for fuel and to build wagons, bridges, furniture, and log cabins. Today, 50 percent of Pennsylvania is still covered in trees, most of which are eastern hemlocks. It was selected as the state tree in 1931.

STATE BIRD: RUFFED GROUSE

The ruffed grouse, also called a partridge, lives wild in the woods. The ruffed grouse was an important source of food for early Pennsylvanians because there were so many of them. The state chose the ruffed grouse as the state bird in 1931.

The ruffed grouse has red-brown plumage and feathery legs. Males make a drumming sound with their wings during mating season.

STATE MAMMAL: WHITE-TAILED DEER

Native Americans and settlers in Pennsylvania hunted white-tailed deer for food, clothing, and shelter. In 1721 the Pennsylvania House of Representatives passed the nation's first game laws, which limited hunting. Hunting laws protect the deer population, which otherwise

White-tailed deer still live throughout Pennsylvania, some weighing as much as 350 pounds.

could die out. The white-tailed deer became the state mammal in 1959.

STATE DOG: GREAT DANE

In 1965 the Pennsylvania government voted on the state dog. All those who wanted the Great Dane, stood up and yipped, growled, and barked. The Speaker of the House, who was running the meeting, announced that the "arfs have it!" The Great Dane won and this "Barking Dog Vote" became a unique moment in legislative history.

This strong, hard-working dog was a favorite among early Pennsylvanians. The Great Dane was so popular that even William Penn owned one.

STATE INSECT: FIREFLY

Most Pennsylvanians call fireflies "lightning bugs." So when the firefly became state insect, some citizens confused it with the pesky blackfly. To stop the confusion, the General Assembly rewrote the law in 1988 using the firefly's **Latin** name, *poturis pensylvanica de geer*.

A firefly is a winged beetle that flies at night. When special cells under the firefly's belly react with oxygen in the air, those cells produce a bright blinking light.

STATE FOSSIL: TRILOBITE

The *phacops rana*, or trilobite, was a small water animal that lived 250 million years ago. It became the state

fossil in 1988, thanks to an elementary school science class. When the students learned that trilobites once lived all over Pennsylvania, they sent letters to the state government asking that it become official.

STATE FISH: BROOK TROUT

The shiny gray brook trout is the only trout native to Pennsylvania. These popular fish swim in the state's 4,000 miles of cold water streams. The trout became the state fish in 1970.

STATE BEVERAGE: MILK

Pennsylvania's dairy farms are the second-largest producer of ice cream in the country. And milk is another major product for the state. Though other states produce milk, too, in 1982 the state government wanted to recognize this favorite beverage.

PENNSYLVANIA STATE QUARTER

In 1999 the U.S. Mint began a program to make quarters from 50 states to celebrate the creation of the United States. Quarters were minted in the order that the states joined the union. Pennsylvania became the second state quarter to be released, because it was the second state to join the Union, in 1787.

The quarter shows the shape of Pennsylvania's rectangular borders. The figure pictured represents liberty and stands next to the state motto: "Virtue, Liberty, and Independence."

Pennsylvania's History and People

William Penn had a dream. In England, as a member of the Quaker religion, he was not allowed to freely practice his faith. So he dreamed of creating a community where people of all religions and backgrounds could live together in peace. Charles II, the king of England, owed money to Penn's father. As payment, he granted Penn a piece of land west of Delaware. This land, with its rolling hills covered in trees, was first called Penn's Woods. It later became known as Pennsylvania, taken from *sylvania*, the Latin word for "woods."

EARLY PENNSYLVANIA

Present-day Pennsylvania was already home to 15,000 native Americans of the Algonquian, Iroquois, Shawnee, and Lenni Lenape tribes. William Penn respected the native people and did not fight with them. In 1681 he wrote a letter of friendship and peace to local Native Americans and granted the Lenni Lenape land west of Philadelphia.

Penn shaped Pennsylvania's early government. He made laws, sold land, and collected taxes. Still, a written policy

According to legend, William Penn and the Lenni Lenape tribe met under an elm tree in Shackamaxon to sign a peace treaty. But despite Penn's help, the Lenape's land borders were often challenged. After Penn died, the Lenape were forced off most of their land.

The Underground Railroad

The Underground Railroad was a network of people who helped slaves find freedom in the North and Canada. Pennsylvania was anti-slavery. In 1688, the first American public protest against slavery took place in the Germantown Friends (Quaker) Meeting House. In 1790, Pennsylvania passed the first state law outlawing slavery. Philadelphia became a central meeting point for the **abolitionists** in the free northeastern states.

Joining the crusade was Harriet Tubman (1819–1913). Born enslaved in Maryland, Tubman was eventually smuggled over the **Mason-Dixon line,** and taken to Philadelphia. She soon became a "conductor" on the railroad to help others. Despite the Fugitive Slave Law of 1850, which punished anyone who helped slaves run away, Tubman stayed strong. She made 19 trips from Philadelphia to the South and helped 300 slaves find freedom.

was needed. In 1701 he approved the Charter of Privileges. This charter said that government should be for the people. Laws should be made in the best interests of the people, and the people must respect and obey those laws. Specifically, the charter gave power to an elected governor and council, plus appointed judges.

Like Pennsylvania, other colonies were becoming more prosperous in the 1700s. Even though they were under England's rule and paid taxes to the king, colonists were not sure what they were getting in return. People began talking about independence from England.

PENNSYLVANIA AND THE AMERICAN REVOLUTION

In 1774 leaders from different colonies met in Philadelphia to discuss politics. Though not everyone agreed, many colonists felt that it was time to break away from England. After much debate, Thomas Jefferson (1743–1826), with help from Benjamin Franklin, John Adams, Roger Sherman, and Robert Livingston, began writing the Declaration of Independence. This document sounded much like Penn's charter. It said that a govern-

Pennsylvania was the second colony to vote for the Constitution. It officially became the second state in 1787.

ment must always serve its people. But the Declaration went one step further. It also said that if a government (such as the King) abuses its power, then the people have a right to challenge it. On July 4, 1776, the Declaration of Independence was adopted and sent to England. England did not give up America without a fight. The American Revolutionary War (1775–1783) began. The people of Pennsylvania saw their share of battles, including the American defeat at Brandywine Creek (1777) and the victory at Valley Forge (1777–1778).

When the war came to an end, the new country had won its independence from Great Britain. But without Great Britain's rule, a new government was needed. In 1787, once again, the leaders of the day met in Philadelphia. They chose Philadelphia because it was a modern city with excellent roads, sidewalks, theaters, and newspapers.

The Congress created a constitution, or plan of government. This constitution recognized that each state had its own government, but above the states would be a federal government. There would be a president, but the president would have to work with Congress to make a law. On December 12, 1787, Pennsylvania ratified, or approved, the new constitution. It became the second state to join the Union.

PENNSYLVANIA AND THE NEW NATION

The Battle of Gettysburg, called the turning point of the **Civil War** (1861–1865), raged for three days—July 1 to July 3, 1863. Union troops won a clear victory at Gettysburg, Pennsylvania—one of the bloodiest battles of the war. Because of this victory, the Confederate army did not again try to invade the North. During the Civil War, Pennsylvania supported the anti-slavery Union troops of the North.

In the second half of the 1800s, Pennsylvania helped drive the Industrial Revolution. The state's factories brought waves of immigrants and created many jobs. Today, Pennsylvania continues to change. But no matter how big the world gets, Pennsylvania's ideas can stay true. Pennsylvania is still a place where all religions and cultures can live together in peace.

FAMOUS PEOPLE FROM PENNSYLVANIA

Benjamin Franklin (1706–1790), colonial leader. Although born in Boston, he made Philadelphia his home. A writer, scientist, and inventor, Franklin was also a wise political leader. He encouraged other colonists to think about independence from England.

Betsy Ross (1752–1836), flag maker and seamstress. Ross and her husband John ran an upholstery business in Philadelphia. She sewed clothes, sofa fabrics, and flags for the Pennsylvania Navy. Lore has it that George Washington visited Ross in June 1776 and asked her to make a flag for the new country. Ross supposedly sug-

The thirteen stripes of the new flag stood for the thirteen colonies. The circle of thirteen stars represented how the colonies were forming a new constellation called the United States. You can see the original design in Betsy Ross's house in downtown Philadelphia.

gested a design, Washington gave her a sketch, and the rest is history.

Richard Allen (1760–1831), religious leader. Born enslaved in Philadelphia, Allen died a free man who had helped change the future for African Americans. From 1780 to 1786, and with the help of his owner, Allen saved money and bought his freedom. Because he was not always welcome in white churches, in 1794 he started a separate Methodist church for African Americans, called the Bethel African Church. This church was successful, but it still depended on white leaders for money. In 1816, to break completely free, Allen began the first independent black church in North America, the new African Methodist Episcopal (AME) church.

Robert Fulton (1765–1815), inventor. As a a teenager in Little Britain (now called Fulton), Fulton was fascinated by machines. As an adult, he invented machines that improved canals and submarines. In 1807 Fulton launched the *Clermont*. His steamboat sailed up the river and against the current from New York City to Albany on the Hudson River.

The Clermont's *first trip covered 150 miles at a speed of 5 miles per hour. This may seem slow to us, but back then it was impressive.*

James Buchanan (1791–1868), politician. Buchanan is the nation's only president from Pennsylvania. In 1857 voters elected this experienced politician as the fifteenth president of the United States. The only unmarried president, Buchanan brought his orphaned niece, Harriet Lane, to the White House as his First Lady.

Mary Cassatt (1845–1926), painter. Cassatt was from Allegheny County but she lived in France when she was in her 20s. She became one of the most celebrated painters of her day and is best known for her paintings of parents and children.

Elizabeth Jane Cochran (1864–1922), journalist. Cochran is best known by her **pen name,** Nellie Bly. Born in Cochran's Mills, Bly was a journalist who wrote mostly about the struggles of poor working girls, such as factory workers. In 1888, for a New York newspaper, she committed herself to a mental hospital for ten days to report on the conditions there. Her report, "Ten Days in a Mad-House," caused a public uproar and led to better treatment of patients with mental illness.

Mary Cassatt's portraits capture a sense of gentleness and joy. She is still revered and studied today.

George C. Marshall (1880–1959), political leader. Marshall came from a working-class family in Uniontown and spent his career in the U.S. military. As chief of staff for President Franklin Roosevelt, Marshall helped lead the U.S. Army to victory in **World War II** (1939–1945). After the war, he became secretary of state for President Harry Truman. Under Truman, he proposed the Marshall Plan, which urged European nations to work together to rebuild. In 1953 Marshall won the **Nobel Peace Prize** for his plan.

Margaret Mead (1901–1978), **anthropologist.** Mead studied how humans are affected by the world around them. In 1925 she went to Samoa, an island in the Pacific Ocean, to see how young girls differed from young girls in the United States. She found that Samoans had less stress and tension even though they lacked modern conveniences, such as grocery stores, radios, or even electricity. Mead published her research in *Coming of Age in Samoa.* She wrote that the more we understand each other, the more we can create positive change in the world.

Marian Anderson (1902–1993), singer. At age 23, Anderson won the chance to sing with the New York Philharmonic Orchestra, which led to concert performances all over the world. In 1939 the **Daughters of the American Revolution** refused to let her sing in their concert hall because she was African American. First Lady **Eleanor Roosevelt** (1884–1962) protested. She resigned her membership in that organization and offered Anderson the Lincoln Memorial as a stage. Anderson performed for 75,000 people that Easter morning, while millions of others heard it broadcast on the radio.

Rachel Carson (1907–1964), scientist, environmentalist, writer. The Springdale-born Carson brought attention to environmental issues. In her famous 1962 book, *Silent Spring*, she

Rachel Carson founded the modern environmental movement.

warned against using **pesticides** in farming. She researched these toxic chemicals and found they stayed in water, in soil, and in the body for many years. They made people and plants sick and stopped birds from having babies. She urged people to use pesticides less. Her research angered the chemical companies that stood to lose millions of dollars, but Carson continued to speak out. For the first time, people learned about the negative effects of pesticides, and many farmers stopped using them.

Bill Cosby (1937–), actor, comedian, author. Cosby is best known for his role on the family sitcom *The Cosby Show,* but he has performed comedy, acted for television and movies, and written books.

Tara Lipinski (1982–), skater. At age three, Lipinski started on roller skates, but at age six switched to blades

and hit the Philadelphia ice rinks. After years of training and competing, her career reached its peak in Nagano, Japan. In the 1998 winter Olympics she became the youngest woman ever to win the gold medal in women's figure skating.

· ·

In 1998 fifteen-year-old Lipinski was the youngest woman in Olympic history to win a gold medal in any individual sport.

Hershey: Chocolatetown, USA

When you hear the word "Hershey," you probably think "chocolate." But Hershey is also the name of a town, an amusement park, a factory, a school—and of the man behind all of them.

MILTON HERSHEY BUILDS HIS DREAM

Milton S. Hershey was born September 13, 1857, on a farm near Derry Church. Hershey first got his sweet tooth while working as a candy and ice cream maker's **apprentice** in Lancaster. At the age of eighteen, he started a candy company of his own. Although his first business—and a few more—failed, Hershey would not give up. In 1883, he opened the Lancaster Caramel Company, which was a huge success.

Lancaster Caramel Company was unique because Hershey used fresh milk in his recipes, while other U.S. companies used dried milk. This made his caramels smoother and creamier. Before long, Hershey experimented with milk to create another candy: milk chocolate. Although milk chocolate was already available in Switzerland and Germany, Hershey was the first to manufacture it in the United States.

During the Great Depression in the 1930s, most Americans could not find jobs. Hershey never laid off a single worker. He hired workers to build a grand hotel, two theaters, and a sports arena, creating work for many families.

In 1900 Hershey sold the Lancaster Caramel Company and used the money to build the world's largest chocolate manufacturing plant, in Derry Church. He planned to **mass-produce** milk chocolate for the first time in the United States. He used machines to make large amounts of chocolate quickly rather than making it all by hand.

HERSHEY PARK MAKES LIFE SWEETER

Hershey's chocolate quickly became popular. His five-cent "Great American Chocolate Bars" made him a wealthy man. But Hershey believed there was more to life than money. He wanted his workers to have good lives, so he built a community around his factory. He built houses, a **trolley** system, and public schools. And for fun, he built a park.

It eventually included a bandstand, swimming pool, bowling alleys, a scenic train ride, and a carousel. In 1915 nearly 200,000 visitors had traveled to Hershey to spend time in his park. When Hershey died in 1945, the sale of his remaining possessions raised only $20,000 because he had given so much of his millions to the town and the school.

Milton Hershey School: Hope for Kids

Milton Hershey and his wife Catherine ("Kitty") loved kids, so they established a place in 1909 where orphan boys could eat, sleep, and go to classes for free. In 1910 the first four boys arrived.

Hershey always said that the school was Kitty's idea, but he kept it going even after she died. In 1918 he gave all his money to the school. Today, this school welcomes girls, children of all races, and those in need. More than 1,000 students attend classes from kindergarten through twelfth grade.

Pennsylvania's State Government

The Pennsylvania state constitution is a plan for the state's government. It provides for three branches of government, just like the U.S. government. The legislative branch creates laws, the executive branch enforces the laws, and the judicial branch applies the laws or interprets those laws. People from all three branches meet in Harrisburg to govern the state.

LEGISLATIVE BRANCH

The General Assembly of the legislative branch creates laws. The General Assembly is divided into two houses. The house of representatives has 203 members who serve two-year terms each. The senate has 50 members who serve four-year terms each. No one can serve more than two terms in a row.

When a representative suggests an idea for a new law, it is called a bill. If the majority of both houses agree on the bill, the governor signs it, and the law becomes official 60 days later. If the governor does not agree with a bill, he or she has ten days to **veto** it. The law will be blocked unless two-thirds of both the House and the Senate override the governor's veto.

EXECUTIVE BRANCH

The governor is the leader of the executive branch and is elected by Pennsylvania citizens. He or she must be at least 30 years old, a U.S. citizen, and a legal resident of Pennsylvania for at least seven years. Once elected, the governor serves a four-year term and can serve only two terms in a row. The governor has the power to appoint other state officials, such as **commissioners** of education, agriculture, or labor. He or she also commands the state police.

In 2003 Edward G. Rendell (1944–) became Pennsylvania's 45th governor. Though he grew up in New York, Rendell went to college and law school in Pennsylvania, and has spent much of his career working for the state.

Each time a new governor is elected, so is a lieutenant governor. The lieutenant governor is president of the state Senate and the governor's closest aide. Other elected officials include the attorney general, who heads the Department of Justice; the auditor general, who oversees the state's plans for spending; and the state treasurer, who keeps track of the state budget.

JUDICIAL BRANCH

The Pennsylvania judicial branch is responsible for interpreting the state's laws.

The system is made up of four levels of courts. Every legal case—from robberies to traffic tickets—is first heard in the lower courts of a city or district by a local judge. If the lower court's decision is challenged, the case is **appealed** in the commonwealth court or superior court. Here, higher judges who represent the state review the decision and either keep it or change it. If the decision is still challenged, the highest court in the state, the Supreme Court, makes the final decision.

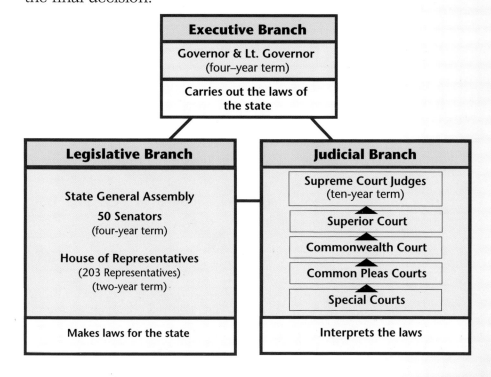

Executive Branch

Governor & Lt. Governor
(four–year term)

Carries out the laws of the state

Legislative Branch

State General Assembly

50 Senators
(four-year term)

House of Representatives
(203 Representatives)
(two-year term)

Makes laws for the state

Judicial Branch

Supreme Court Judges
(ten-year term)

Superior Court

Commonwealth Court

Common Pleas Courts

Special Courts

Interprets the laws

The gold-domed capitol in Harrisburg was completed in 1906.

Seven judges, or justices, are elected to the Pennsylvania Supreme Court. Each justice serves a ten-year term and can be reelected an unlimited number of times. The justice who has served the longest without a break is automatically the chief justice.

Pennsylvania's State Constitutions

Pennsylvania's laws changed over the years. It is important that a state's laws represent the best interests of the state. Below are some of the more significant details.

Constitution	Year Adopted	What It Said
First State Constitution	1776	Instead of a governor, a group of people (called the executive council) would lead the colony. Before, only people who had property could vote. Now, people did not need to own land in order to vote.
Second State Constitution	1790	The legislators changed their mind on one issue: they decided they needed a governor after all. The executive council was replaced.
Third State Constitution	1838	For many years, the people who supported the government were appointed by other politicians. Now, many of these officials are elected by the people of Pennsylvania. This gives the people a stronger voice.
Fourth State Constitution	1873	Legislators could no longer pass amendments—make changes—to the constitution by themselves. The changes have to be approved by both the house and the senate, and the people of Pennsylvania need to vote on it.

Pennsylvania's Culture

Pennsylvania is a melting pot of many cultures. In the 1700s and 1800s, Swedes, Native Americans, Scottish, and Germans known as Pennsylvania Dutch worked the land. The Pennsylvania Dutch actually have German backgrounds. When they first arrived in Pennsylvania, they would use the German word for "German," which was "Deutsch." "Deutsch" became pronounced "Dutch" and soon that's how they were known.

Today, culture can be found in the smells of garlic cooking in the Italian South Side of Philadelphia. Or the salsa music heard in Allentown's Puerto Rican neighborhoods. Or in the **gospel music** of a Pittsburgh Baptist church. This diverse mix of people still influences Pennsylvania's foods, religions, and traditions.

A UNIQUE PARADE

The New Year's Day Mummers Parade in Philly is a unique Pennsylvania event. Having started in 1901, it is one of the oldest continuous folk festivals in the country.

The simple life of the Amish is part of Pennsylvania's unique culture.

The Mummers are divided into four groups: Comic, Fancy, String, and Fancy Brigade. Some costumes are so elaborate, they take up to a year to create.

Mumme is a German word for "mask," but the Mummers draw from several cultures. Before William Penn arrived, the area called Pennsylvania today had a large Swedish population. One Swedish tradition was to paint faces, dress in costumes, and visit friends the day after Christmas. The English settlers later introduced "mummers plays" featuring dancing, sword fights, and comedy.

Every year 25,000 Mummers in Philadelphia wear costumes covered with sequins, mirrors, and ostrich feathers. Some costumes weigh as much as 150 pounds! Early New Year's morning, the Mummers dance down Philadelphia's Broad Street. Numerous bands play everything: accordions, saxophones, drums, violins, banjos, bass fiddles, **glockenspiels**, and clarinets.

MUSEUMS

Andy Warhol (1928–1987) was an important figure in American art. He drew pictures of familiar things or people—such as a Campbell's soup can or Marilyn Monroe—and turned them into huge, colorful **silkscreen** paintings. Warhol's work is in museums all over the world. But the only place dedicated to him is the Andy Warhol Museum in his hometown of Pittsburgh.

Another special museum is the National Liberty Museum. It celebrates the nation's promise of freedom and liberty for all people. Exhibits honor those who help make the world a better place, including the African leader Nelson Mandela and the firefighters of September 11, 2001.

Pennsylvania's Food

Pennsylvania has all kinds of tempting foods: Philly cheesesteaks, the Pittsburgh Clark Bar, and funnel cake. But one of the biggest influences on local food comes from the Pennsylvania Dutch.

FOOD OF THE PENNSYLVANIA DUTCH

Pennsylvania Dutch foods are hearty, home-cooked foods that Pennsylvanians say "stick to your ribs." Many people of German heritage eat pork and **sauerkraut** on New Year's Day to bring good luck for the coming year. Or how about some *Groescht Weshhinkel* (growsht-VEH-shink-ul) *und* (unt) *Gruumbiere Sas (GROOM-bee-ur-zahs) mit Dippy?* That is a mouthful...both to say and to eat! It is actually just roast turkey with mashed potatoes and gravy.

Pretzels are also popular. Pretzels originated in Germany, and the Pennsylvania Dutch brought them to the United States. In 1861 Julius Sturgis opened the first commercial pretzel bakery in the United States. Located in Lititz, the company still uses its original 150-year-old ovens to make soft pretzels.

One Pennsylvania Dutch group is the Amish. The Amish live very simple lives, without electricity or other modern luxuries. Though the Amish also live in Ohio and other states, a large population calls Lancaster, Pennsylvania, home.

Want to top off your dinner with something sweet? Spoon some fresh apple butter on a piece of bread, or dig into some *Shnitz 'n Knepp*, or apple dumplings. On the Tuesday before **Lent** begins, a *fastnacht* fresh from the oven is a special treat.

Shoo-fly Pie

It is hard to explain what shoo-fly pie tastes like. It is so sweet that if you put one on a windowsill to cool, flies are sure to gather.

Ingredients

2/3 cup hot water

1/2 teaspoon baking soda

2/3 cup molasses

1 egg

a 9-inch unbaked pastry shell

1 cup all-purpose flour

2/3 cup brown sugar

6 tablespoons butter or margarine, cut into pieces

Be sure to have an adult help you! Turn on the oven to 350°F. In a medium bowl, mix the hot water and baking soda. Stir until the baking soda is dissolved. Beat in the molasses and the egg. Pour the whole mix into the pastry shell and set aside. In a different bowl, mix the flour, sugar, and butter with a fork until it turns into crumbs. Sprinkle about two thirds of the crumbs over your pie, leaving the rest for later. Bake the pie for 40 minutes, then carefully take it out of the oven and sprinkle the rest of your crumbs onto the top. Put the pie back in the oven for 15 more minutes. Then take it out and let it cool for about an hour.

Pennsylvania's Folklore and Legends

Common customs, art, music, dances, and stories are often called folklore. The following folk stories are special to Pennsylvania.

WOLVES AND DOGS: NOT THE BEST OF FRIENDS

A local Native American legend helps explain why wolves and dogs do not get along.

A long time ago, wolves and dogs were friends. One winter a wolf was particularly cold and hungry. He said to his dog companion, "Who will go to the humans and bring back fire so we can make our own fire?" The dog replied, "I will get some fire, my friend!" And off he went in search of where the Delaware people lived.

When the little dog got near the fire, a young girl noticed him. She thought the dog was so cute that she went over to pet him. She said, "Come here. You are cold! I will feed you meat and bread."

Well, since the dog was cold and hungry, he was happy to follow the girl into her house made of bark. Soon, he forgot to bring fire back to his friend, the wolf. The wolf waited and waited but eventually gave up. He was hurt because he thought his friend was a liar. He ran to find fire somewhere else. Perhaps if he had been invited into a house of bark, he would have stayed, too. But to this day, wolves are not friends with dogs.

Hex Signs for Good Luck

When Germans came to Pennsylvania, they brought their own language, customs, and crafts. One unique design that shows up on Pennsylvania Dutch barns, bibles, quilts, and furniture is the six-pointed star design, called a hex. The German word for it is *sechs*, but the English-speaking neighbors thought it sounded like "hex." The new name stuck. Those who believe in hexes say they bring luck if the owner works hard.

Traditional designs are painted by hand. The star design is always in a circle, with the middle symbolizing God. The drawings around the circle symbolize the special areas of a person's life:

- Hearts = love
- Tulips = faith
- Oak leaves and acorns = strength
- Eagles = strength and protection
- Birds (or *distelfinks*) = luck and happiness

The colors of the hex have meaning. Blue is for protection. White is for staying good-hearted. Green means plenty of food and success. Red stands for strong emotions, such as love and happiness.

Pennsylvania's Sports Teams

Pennsylvania covers all the major sports, with major-league professional football, baseball, basketball and hockey teams in Philadelphia and Pittsburgh. College sports are also popular, especially at Penn State University.

FOOTBALL

The Philadelphia Eagles and Pittsburgh Steelers, both part of the National Football League (NFL), have strong football traditions. The Eagles have won three NFL championships and played in the Super Bowl once. The Steelers have won four Super Bowl titles.

Called the Cradle of Quarterbacks, western Pennsylvania has produced NFL quarterbacks Jim Kelly, Joe Montana, Dan Marino, Joe Namath, and Johnny Unitas. All of them are in the Pro Football Hall of Fame—and have eleven Super Bowl appearances among them.

BASEBALL

Pennsylvania baseball has a long history. The Philadelphia Phillies, formed in 1883, is the oldest professional

The Pittsburgh Steelers play their games at Heinz field, which can hold thousands of cheering fans.

Go Nittany Lions!

Every week in the fall, thousands head to State College, Pennsylvania, to cheer on the Penn State Nittany Lions. Under Joe Paterno, Penn State's coach since 1966, the football team has thrived. Paterno has guided them to two national college football championships. He has won more than 350 games. He has coached Penn State for more than 50 years—more than 600 games! He won "Coach of the Year" four times, and he was the first football coach ever to be named "Sportsman of the Year" by *Sports Illustrated* magazine.

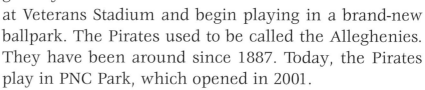

sports team to never stop playing, never change cities, and never change its name. In 2004 the Phillies will say good-bye to their home field at Veterans Stadium and begin playing in a brand-new ballpark. The Pirates used to be called the Alleghenies. They have been around since 1887. Today, the Pirates play in PNC Park, which opened in 2001.

HOCKEY

The National Hockey League (NHL) Pittsburgh Penguins won two Stanley Cup Championships with Mario Lemieux. Lemieux was one of the greatest players of all time and is in the NHL Hall of Fame.

The NHL's Philadelphia Flyers was not the city's first professional hockey team. In the 1930s the Philadelphia Quakers wore the traditional orange-and-black colors.

Pennsylvania's Businesses and Products

Over the years Pennsylvania's economy has thrived on agriculture, mining, manufacturing, and transportation. This is still true, though more businesses today focus on professional services and tourism.

FARM PRODUCTS

In the 1700s, Pennsylvania was called "the breadbasket of America" because of its plentiful farms. Today nine million **acres** are still farmed. Dairy products, eggs, and cattle are most important, followed by corn, buckwheat, mushrooms, and apples. Pennsylvania is also one of the nation's leading Christmas tree growers. Second only to Oregon, Pennsylvania has more than 1,400 tree farms.

Pennsylvania is the second largest producer of ice cream and frozen dairy products in the United States. Lancaster County, in the southeast, has more dairy farms than any other county in the state.

Bethlehem Steel is the country's second largest steel producer. They shipped 8.5 million tons of steel products in 2000.

MINING AND MANUFACTURING

Pennsylvania's land is rich in natural resources such as oil, natural gas, iron ore, limestone, slate, clay, and sand. However, the state has more anthracite coal, or hard coal, than any other state. Anthracite is important because it burns cleaner than soft coal, with almost no smoke and ashes. Nearly 100 billion tons of coal are still waiting to be mined.

The Pennsylvania steel industry was successful because the state had plenty of coal to fuel factories and lots of iron ore to make steel. With companies such as U.S. Steel, in Pittsburgh, and Bethlehem Steel, in Bethlehem, Pennsylvania has been the nation's leader. Today about nine million tons of steel are still shipped each year to other states and other countries. The steel is used for construction of buildings, vehicles, and cargo containers.

Pennsylvania also manufactures cement, paper, and processed foods. The Heinz company, which makes pickles, ketchup, and other familiar foods, is one of the world's largest food-processing companies. Another big company, Alcoa, which produces aluminum for everything from tin cans to cars, is the largest maker of aluminum in the world.

SERVICE INDUSTRIES

Many people in Pennsylvania work in professional industries. Pittsburgh is the headquarters of PNC, which is one

The Crayola Factory

The Crayola® Factory in Easton, Pennsylvania, is the number one crayon maker in the world. In 1900 Edwin W. Binney ran a branch of the Binney & Smith company in Easton through a partnership with his nephew, C. Harold Smith. First Binney made art materials, including pencils and chalk. In 1903, he created the Crayola company.

Today, families and school students visit the Crayola Discovery Center in downtown Easton. They discover the mystery behind magic markers, sidewalk chalk, and silly putty. And they watch how crayons are made. A factory display shows a rainbow of hot wax streaming into crayon-shaped molds. The cooled sticks are wrapped in colorful paper, and each person gets to take a fresh box home.

of the nation's twenty largest bank corporations. The city is also the headquarters for Charles Schwab, a billion-dollar investment company. Meanwhile, Philadelphia is home to the oldest U.S. **stock exchange**: the PHLX (Philadelphia Stock Exchange).

Education also plays a part in the economy. The state has more than 200 colleges and universities. The University of Pennsylvania runs the nation's oldest medical school. Founded in 1765 by Benjamin Franklin, it was the first medical school to mix classroom lectures with hands-on experience bedside teaching.

Attractions and Landmarks

There is much to do and see in Pennsylvania. Visitors can relive U.S. history, ride a roller coaster, or relax in the mountains.

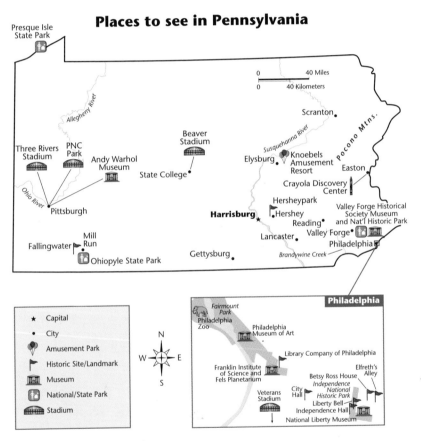

Places to see in Pennsylvania

HISTORICAL SITES

Philadelphia is full of history from Colonial America. Independence National Historic Park is the site of Independence Hall where the Declaration of Independence and the U.S. Constitution were signed. Just eighteen miles outside Philadelphia is Valley Forge National Historic Park. This was where George Washington and his Continental Army camped during the cold winter of 1777–1778. The winds off the Susquhanna River were brutal. And temperatures ranged only from 6 to 16°F. Back then, the site was covered with log huts, cattle pens, and ditches. Today, it is covered with walking trails, grassy fields, and the Valley Forge Historical Society Museum. Also on the grounds is

George Washington's statue stands in front of Independence Hall.

Washington's headquarters, where Washington lived with his wife Martha throughout that terrible winter.

Gettysburg, in central Pennsylvania, is the largest battlefield shrine in the United States. It was here that the only **Civil War** (1861–1865) battle north of Maryland was fought. More than 1,000 monuments cover 40 miles of land to honor this bloody and brave fight.

About 12,000 soldiers camped at Valley Forge, braving cold winds and snow. Two thousand men died from diseases such as pneumonia.

In 1752 the Philadelphia Liberty Bell cracked—the very first time it was rung! Its replacement lasted close to 100 years but cracked in 1846.

THE GREAT OUTDOORS

Presque Isle—in French, "almost an island"—is an ever-changing **peninsula** off of Lake Erie. This seven-mile stretch of land is the only surf beach in Pennsylvania. The winds that rise off Lake Erie contribute to the rolling waves that are usually only seen near an ocean.

JUST FOR FUN

Knoebels (kah-NO-bulls) Amusement Resort, in Elysburg, takes classic rides from parks that have shut down and reassembles them like new. That means Knoebels has rides available nowhere else. For instance, it has two carousels with handpainted wooden horses that date back more than 50 years.

Fallingwater

Frank Lloyd Wright (1867–1959), a famous American architect, believed a building should become a part of the natural environment. One of Wright's houses, called Fallingwater, fits right into its surroundings.

In Mill Run, built right into the side of the mountain and hanging directly over Bear Run waterfalls, is Fallingwater. When you walk inside, you feel like you are still outside. Wright built so many windows that you can almost touch the trees. And there are places in the floor where you can look directly into a creek.

Map of Pennsylvania

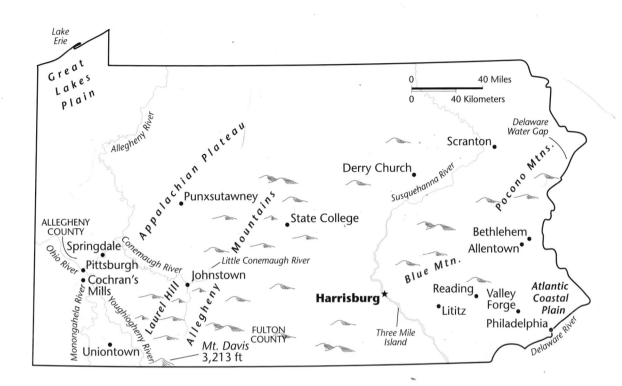

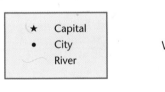

★ Capital
• City
River

Glossary

abolitionists people who were opposed to slavery and worked to end slavery in the United States

acre a unit of area used to measure land

anthropologist a person who studies human being and their culture, physical nature and environment

appealed legal decision is transferred from a lower court to a higher court for a review of the lower court's legal decision

apprentice a person who learns a skill by working with an expert in that field

atom invisible building blocks of all things

Civil War (1861–1865) in the U.S., the war between the North and the South

circulating library a library from which the public can borrow books

commissioners people who are given authority to run public services

Daughters of the American Revolution an organization for women descended from early American settlers

Emmy Awards awards given each year for outstanding achievement in television by the Academy of Television Arts and Sciences

endangered when a species is at risk for extinction, or dying out

glockenspiel a musical instrument made of metal bars and played with two small hammers

gospel music a type of music, made popular by African Americans, based on folk music, spirituals, and jazz

Great Depression period of American history in the 1930s when there were very few jobs and little money and food

hibernate to pass the winter resting; an animal's body slows down so that it does not eat as much

Industrial Revolution period in history when machines and factories made work more efficient

keystone a wedge placed at the top of an arch to lock all other pieces in place

Lent Christian season of fast and prayer lasting 40 days between Ash Wednesday and Easter

Mason-Dixon line the boundary between Pennsylvania and Maryland that acted as the division between the southern states that allowed slavery and the northern states that did not

mass-produce to make large quantities using machines

municipal relating to a local government

Nobel Peace Prize an international award given annually to recognize those who have worked for peace

nuclear a type of energy caused by changes in an atom's nucleus

paralysis the loss of ability to move body parts often due to an injury

pen name when a writer uses a different name from his or her own

peninsula land surrounded by water on three sides

pesticides chemicals used to kill pests, especially insects

radiation energy waves transmitted from a radioactive substance

sauerkraut chopped cabbage that is salted and sour-tasting

silkscreen a design made from spraying ink on a silk or mesh fabric

stock exchange a place where stocks and bonds are bought and sold

temperate moderate climate that does not reach extreme cold or heat

trolley a small bus or car that runs on a track

vaccine a medicine that immunizes or protects against disease

veto to reject a bill so that it does not become a law

virus microscopic organism that causes disease

World War II (1939–1945) war in which Great Britain, the U.S., France, China, and the Soviet Union fought and defeated Germany, Italy, and Japan

More Books to Read

Craven, Jean, and Scott Ingram. *Pennsylvania: The Keystone State (World Almanac Library of the States)*. New York: World Almanac Education, 2002.

Heinrichs, Ann. *America the Beautiful: Pennsylvania*. Danbury, Conn.: Children's Press, 2000.

Marsh, Carole. *My First Pocket Guide to Pennsylvania*. Peachtree City, Ga.: Gallopade International, Inc., 2000.

Paul, Lewis M. *Discovering Pennsylvania*. Beaverton, Ore.: American Products Publishing Co., 2001.

Index

About the Author

Susan McCulloch spent her first 26 years living, learning, and working in Pennsylvania. She now works as a managing editor in New York City but often returns to Pennsylvania to visit family and friends.